P9-ECJ-536

FROM ONE LIFE TO ANOTHER

From One Life

University of Pittsburgh Press

TO ANOTHER

Shirley Kaufman

Published by the University of Pittsburgh Press, Pittsburgh, Pa. 15260

Feffer and Simons, Inc., London
Manufactured in the United States of America

Library of Congress Cataloging in Publication Data

Kaufman, Shirley.
From one life to another.

(Pitt poetry series)
I. Title.
PS3561.A862F7 811'.5'4 78-23502
ISBN 0-8229-3390-X
ISBN 0-8229-5300-5 pbk.

Grateful acknowledgment is made to the editors of the following magazines for permission to reprint poems that first appeared there: *Choice, Field, Ironwood, Kayak, The Massachusetts Review, Midstream, The Nation, Out of Sight,* and *Poetry Northwest*.

"Colors" and "From Here to There" first appeared in *The Ohio Review*.

Letter 2 of "Letters from the Snow" was originally published as "A Letter from the Snow," © 1975 The New Yorker Magazine, Inc.

The last section of the long poem "Divorce" was published in *The Massachusetts Review* and titled "Divorce."

Most of the sections in "Letting Go" and "Divorce" were published in an earlier version in *Field.*

"Looking at Henry Moore's Elephant Skull Etchings in Jerusalem During the War" appeared first in *Field,* and was published as a book with the etchings of Henry Moore by Unicorn Press, Greensboro, N.C., 1977.

"Dinosaur Tracks in Beit Zayit" appears in *Fifty Contemporary Poets: The Creative Process,* edited by Alberta T. Turner, © 1977 by Longman Inc.

"The Mountain" appears in *Tangled Vines: A Collection of Mother and Daughter Poems,* edited by Lyn Lifshin, Beacon Press, Boston, 1978.

"The Mountain," "Take Anything" (in an earlier version), "Loving," and "Looking at Henry Moore's Elephant Skull Etchings in Jerusalem During the War" were taped in Black Box 11, The New Classroom, 1976, for audio serial publication.

The author wishes to express her gratitude to Mrs. Eleanor Torrey West of Ossabaw Island where some of these poems were written.

To Bill

The publication of this book is supported by a grant from the National Endowment for the Arts in Washington, D.C., a Federal agency.

CONTENTS

I From One Life
Horseshoe Crabs 3
Shells 5
Bunk Beds 6
The Rooms Are Smaller When You Return 9
Colors 11
Lawrence at Taos 12
T'ai Chi 15
America 17
Come Back 18
From Here to There 19

II To Another
Adam 23
Leah 24
Tracking 26
Letting Go 27
Divorce 32
Letters from the Snow 38
The Words 41
Loving 43

III Starting Over
Starting Over 47
The Way 48
Looking at Henry Moore's Elephant Skull
Etchings in Jerusalem During the War 49
Reruns 55

Dinosaur Tracks in Beit Zayit 56
Take Anything 58
Meeting 62
The Mountain 64
Thinking About the Future of Jerusalem 67
The Next Step 68

I From One Life

HORSESHOE CRABS

She is astonished by the moon
as she crawls out of the sea
on a small island, dragging
the male crab on her tail.

He hangs there by the hooks
he's just grown out of his legs,
clutching at what she
offers him, and half her size.

She wears him as she wears
her great shell like a mask
stretched over her body
and the steaming eggs.

Air enters her gills
like moonlight
and she breathes it on this
one night out of the water

with her sisters, and their
ferocious lovers
hanging on. Already
the tide slips back,

and on the beach the crabs
are giddy, meaning to go.
They always mean to.
Four hundred million years

of habit, still they are caught
like shards left over
when the roof falls in.
They lie at sunrise

in the bright sand, holding
the dark inside them,
dreaming of floors of oceans
where they move alone.

Ossabaw Island
May, 1977

SHELLS

Some time after you're forty
when you say you'd like to
forget, you mean you wish
you remembered where you
ate dinner, or what you were
reading, or the name of the place
you stayed in near the Ponte Vecchio.

You know you've seen
that face in the crowd,
the eyes look after you
mildly out of another life,
but where?

The sky flashes with light
as if a great pit opened behind
the hills boiling with fire,
but then the rain comes
and you can't be sure.

And on the beach today,
picking up shells
as they lay bleaching along the dunes,
she pressed one to her ear
and said she heard music,
but when she passed it
to you, it was gone.

BUNK BEDS

1

My face in the mirror and his eyes
back of my eyes and back
of us both the money carefully
counted in a purse like licorice
buttons, bottle caps,

or *groszy* in Ulanov, mud
in the streets where you can't
see it, up to your ankles
as you find your way to the river,
lose and find it again.

Poland, whatever they call it
when the borders change,
a river of mud where
nobody fishes, Poland
around you like a swamp.

His brother reads Schiller
by the small lamp
at the toll bridge, all
the unholy books you never
should open. His secret

longing to be keeper
of the bridge like Max,
to read the books in German
stopping the wagons
to collect the tolls.

2

Books and money. Money and never mind
the books. You might say water
under the bridge or mud,
or how do you feed a wife
and child. Telling us money

got him to the next town,
money bought him a coat
that wasn't his brother's, money
peddling eggs from door to door
so he could buy the ticket

to America where there was more
of it in bunk beds
than anyone dreamed. Everything
smelled of varnish even
in spring. He cut the cost

and piled them one on top
of the other like blocks or bricks
or candy bars, like pieces
of dough you play with
till the stuff gets spongy,

doubles in size. You
punch it down and watch it
rise, cinnamon buns,
the Dow Jones, what do you
think? It grows on trees?

3

There in the photographs his smile
suggests what passes for happiness,
the slight blur of his arm
feeling the weight of the biggest
salmon he ever caught.

When he had trouble sleeping
he told me he thought of salmon
on his line, reeling
the big ones in, their scales
in the sun like silver coins.

I hold his hand until
the soft skin tightens with a
jerk and I let go. His head
strains upward and his lips
as if the air is somewhere

beyond his reach, as if
he sucks a pineapple soda
while the small bits of fruit
get stuck in the straw. It is his
death he sucks on and it comes

in quick gasps thicker than
syrup at the bottom of the glass.
His mouth gives up then, open
and round like a young trout, size
of a dollar with the dollar gone.

THE ROOMS ARE SMALLER WHEN YOU RETURN

I dreamed he was dying
and I stayed away. That made me guilty,
everyone looked at me as if to say
poor man and you the only
daughter. I woke too early
with the air wrung out after the rain,

and the feeling they were waiting
behind the fence to see what I'd do.
I stood in the center of the stage
just like they told me,
but when the curtains opened
I forgot my lines.

I dreamed he was dying
and he opened the door of the house
I grew up in: now that you've come
you can decide what you want,
a dollar they'll give us, only
a dollar for her little ring.

He was walking from room to room
with a yellow pad, making
his lists, my mother's accretion
of things he forgot
and called merchandise, figuring
what it would bring.

The rooms are smaller
when you return, and I didn't know
whether to be offended
or to please. Next year was coming
so fast with its own decisions
I couldn't get out of the way.

I wanted to hide
by closing my eyes, to play
the old game where each time I jumped
he'd raise the bar, to put my small feet
on his feet as he carried me to bed.
I dreamed he was dying and he did.

COLORS

for Louis Comtois

I want to enter those great stripes to feel
how the light churns under them.

Colors are the instruments of light,
you said. They give back what we've forgotten

though the proportions change, and when
I step away I find what I've lost.

We keep on drifting, our faces
taking the gray together and that faint

aura of sunrise moving toward day.
So much we see we do not see at all.

How blue the veins are on the hands
of the statue of David through the white skin.

Even the absence of light makes light in the mind.
And colors? After the light is gone?

LAWRENCE AT TAOS

1

She said a white cloud
followed them up the hill
and hovered above the crazy androgynous
phoenix with its plump white breasts
like lids of sugar bowls.

Both of them noticed it
and told each other later.
So I didn't just make it up,
she said. It looked like the soft
underside of an egret's wing.

When they had stood a long time
over his ashes, the cloud
turned into smoke or steam
or shimmeriness, that was the word
she wanted, and was gone.

2

In Taos we eat sopapilla
with honey butter at La Cosina
and pay one dollar to see
the obscene paintings, banned in London,
by the author of *Lady Chatterley's Lover*.

They fly back into paradise
as he kept running through
the gates of the wrong gardens.
He went to Mexico and almost died.
Back to the ranch. But didn't stay.

When Frieda returned to Taos
with his ashes, she forgot them
on the train. They had to
flag the train down at the next stop
to get them back again.

3

Someone keeps looking in the window,
stealing Brett's paintings off the wall,
the drawings she made of him.
The sun's too bright. That's why
her eyes are covered with milk.

She has to be lifted, heavy
lumps of her, into the chair.
She turns up her hearing aid.
Ah Lawrence. Telling us how
she touched him to make him calm.

And she goes on about the cabin,
and the horses dragging the wood in,
Photographs of her quite
beautiful and slender next to a tree
or in a doorway, watching him.

4

A lizard runs over Frieda's tomb,
his green tail longer than the rest
of his body. There are fresh
pine boughs on the ground.
And a visitors' book

full of ecstatic letters
to the dead. Someone pasted
a poem in the little chapel
over two roses in a bottle.
So many women in love,

their souls like small eggs
spilling out of their shells.
Outside the phoenix sweats
in its white plaster,
unable to rise.

T'AI CHI

You get out of bed each morning
and do T'ai Chi.
You feel like clouds, like steam
with its fuzzy little particles.
You scoop up space in your arms
and bend slowly letting it spill.
Circles ripple around you
where you turn on the pin
of your own center,
rain falls
in a puddle of rain.

You tell me the story of the serpent
and the crane. The crane
stabs over and over
with its beak. The snake,
as quick as anything that flies,
curves out of reach.
They each take turns
at yielding.
You want to learn
the perfect balance
of that dance.

Now the dark sockets
of your body yearn
toward perfection.
You feel each disc of your spine
lift
as you rise on the journey
that takes you out
and back again.
You walk on water, softly
the inside of your leg
comes toward you.

Carry tiger to mountain,
grasp the bird's tail.

You do T'ai Chi
without a sound. I watch
how your muscles find
your bones, your intricate
structure being held,
how it can topple
to the ground.

Like hands making shadows
on a wall, you move
your wrists.
There is an unseen ball
you take in your arms
as you step lightly
balancing air, balancing
your breath till it goes
out of you.

AMERICA

If you had some
place to get to

following
the herds thousands

of years walking
over the Bering

Straits how
could you imagine

your own
extinction?

COME BACK

The girl next to me
on the Trailways bus is reading
Modern Man in Search of a Soul.
I'm riding from Springfield
to New York to get
a divorce. My soul
sits on a black wire
trying to be a bird.

Come back sweet thing,
as if it could
hear me or would listen
now that it's busy
with its own redemption.

Everything's fickle.
Even the atom. Its little heavy
heart surrounded by clouds
of electrons. New particles
keep popping faster than anyone
can name them.

And I'm sealed in this bus
with the landscape giving up
its last dependable trees,
and the sun hot on the window
I can't open, and the whole
world rushing from
where it ought to be.

FROM HERE TO THERE

for the De Votis

Lying awake at midnight
and the dark filling my eyes,
I walk again past Willa's tree
and Mark's, maples as old as they
to measure them by,
down to the brook,
the first clusters of violets.
I look into the petals
where the red tongue lies.

It's May, the pine needles
spongy under my shoes,
and Willa takes me where the stream
pours in a steep fall
down to the lower stream.
Mark brings the jar of worms
he dug by flashlight,
and the dogs run with us
under the brush.

It's hard to see them,
they keep fading into the sun
or growing up
in the Massachusetts woods
while everything changes, everything
happens some place else.
Willa helps me name the flowers,
even the ones
we can't be sure of,

and the trees.
We know too much already
I want to tell her
I'm afraid of my own death
more than the end
of the world. We watch the fish
leap out of the water
brilliant as fireworks
when Mark throws his line.

II To Another

ADAM

His sigh
is the first wheel turning
for the one who hears it
and will set everything
in motion.

Neither of them
is ready
but the earth
pulls everything
down from heaven.

Under that ceiling
they can see
God's finger almost
touching Adam's
but not quite.

There's so much
space
between them
that they can't
go back.

LEAH

. . . but Rachel was beautiful . . . .
— Genesis 29:17

I do what I have to
like an obedient daughter
or a dog. Not for your fingers
in my flesh. I watch you
every day as you watch her.
Since I'm the ugly one,
the one pushed into your bed
at night when you can't
tell the difference.

I've got another
son inside me, and still
you watch her. She doesn't
sag as I do after each birth
until you fill me again.

Why can't you look at me
in daylight, or take
my hand and press it
against your mouth?
I'm not a stone, a shell
your foot rolls over
in the sand. The life
gone out of it.
Maybe I am.
Your sons have sucked me
empty and dull.

I leave your tent at dawn
and walk to the river where I
throw my clothes off,
and the water shows me
my body floating
on the surface. It shivers
when I touch the blue dome
of your unborn child.
I touch my unwanted self
where the smooth skin
stretches over my breasts,
the silver veins. I'm cold.

I enter the water
as you enter me. Quick.
Like insects doing it while
they fly. The shock of it
lifts me,
and I swim raging
against the stream.

TRACKING

He has to say
his name when he calls,
as if the voice belonged
to someone I didn't know.

If he had a gun
he would know how to use it.
The man in the Sam Browne belt
from World War II.

I should unbuckle him,
undo the button tenderly
over his throat,
but the hair is grey on his chest

and he's not my child.
His voice settles around my neck.
I look out at the smooth body
of snow. Huge dogs

are tracking it
with their blind paws.

LETTING GO

The pipes froze
there's no more
water in the house
use the outdoors they say

I go through trees
the wet leaves thick
under my feet
small pouches of snow
strange on the California ground

finding a place to squat
ridiculous woman
my ass
            speckled
with cold

*

But then the statue
of the girl in bronze shining
over herself her thumb
pressed in the soft flesh of her waist
the long curve of her neck
and shoulder following the smooth line

down to her elbow her left hand
turning around her calf she is all
rhythm bending to her foot feeling
the run of her blood
under her skin the glow
of her back highlight of the small
rise at the spine's base deep
shade where her buttocks begin

*

So that I hide from old friends
and the museum is full

so that I meet you
easy the fine rain
powders my skin
it will slide off like hair-thin petals
milkweed falling through air

rain
the whole sky in motion
and my face taking it
like a freshness of earth
turned over

*

I will be
weightless
in the blue waves
of your room

or in the sunlight
looking across the tense curve
of the bridge

while you in the vivid foreground
stand
as in a bas-relief

surf whitens your shoulders
and you tell me how
the breakers came at home
crashing over the beaches
and your breath knocked
out of you sometimes
riding them
with your body only

*

What we discover
for the first time

is the thing we've known
having this morning
in another's eyes

or how the sky is
with the bridge
against it

it sways there
slightly
fixed in its own elation

*

You speak of letting go
to hang on

                    running the ship
past saving on the shoals
and the black mass of Koh-ring
towering

                    until he swerves
at the last blink

the nerve of that captain
and his desperate skill

*

Each thrust of our lives
we balk at choices
our bodies change before
we enter them

the mind jumps backward
from the mindless flesh

but the long pull begins
far out at sea
climbing and falling

as a muscle strains
under the skin

veined water
over

          and over

the long breaking
the loud foam

*

Oh the pure seriousness
of pleasure

hum of gas in the oven
on and off on and off
keeping the temperature even

having and giving
darkness

                    and light
around your wrist
like summer
moving between my legs

and out of your eyes
that dark in the last moment
when the wave

lifts

wholly out of itself

*

A kind of listening
beautiful in the half-light
spreading a net to hold my weight
the soft dark hairs

a great space opens
and you pull
me into myself

to come out
lavish on the other side

pool of Siloam

where my breath finds
its way slowly
back from your mouth

like music Scriabin
something else I say
wanting
like
not being able

*

Or how you look
at your breasts
after

how

I don't know
a certain look
what kind
of look

I don't know
proud I think yes
proud

DIVORCE

High over the bridge
the cold air stings
our mouths our breath
comes in white circles

there is a lid of ice
where the ditch runs

you break a sheet of it
hold it a minute
brittle with sun

it shatters
when you toss it in the road

the sky lies drying
on the broken bits

why I didn't say
I broke the mirror too

or invented a puzzle
cracked in sharp little pieces

slivers keep turning up
under my feet

I can't walk around without
my shoes

*

The sun lets itself down
in pale yellow
over the Farralones
small mouth
of a burned-out mountain lost
in the sea

and the city floats
out of the bay
a mirage of long marriage

we can hear only
a deep hum rising
from the bottom
in the cold
where the buildings huddle together

*

Three sandpipers
run on the shore
their skinny feet spread out
in opposite directions

soft white bellies
one jump ahead of the tide

*

Did you ever see
a sea gull like that?
Eyes like watermelon seeds
looking at us
from the table across the deck
catching a french fried potato
in its beak

I used to think the red spot
on its yellow beak
was catsup
all those hamburgers

smug
you say

it's the first bird
in us that makes us think
we know

poor yelling infant
covered with down

*

I had forgotten how I plunged
like a hooked fish

more than I had to
giving birth

I go on looking
for the abundance of pain

that twists my side
like a crank

not yet keep crying
wanting to hold it in

*

Old intricate lives
we are so delicately stitched

peritoneum
three layers of muscle
subcutaneous tissue
skin

each layer
sutured tightly
over the wounds

would you undo that?

*

Perfect small cancers
growing
in perfect
small
bodies
of laboratory mice

quicker than birds
when we reach out to them

their panic

even in the clean
wood shavings

*

We can't figure out
how to fasten the new seat belts

we sit there for hours
in the front seat

trying to put the two ends together
there seems to be nothing

to catch on
or they don't fit

*

You had been talking about
the management of risk
warnings before we turn out
the light check the double locks
set the burglar alarm
don't leave the hose on the street
for someone to trip on

we fumble toward sex
like old men
who repeat the same story
forgetting
repeat it again

if you untie that balloon
it's going to go up
and you'll never get it down

*

Listen I want to explain
there's no nightingale
in our pillows

what strains in our throats
is our own blood

excesses I'm given to
lately

it's the impurities
that color the stone
that ultimate blue-white diamond

did you hear that did you
hear even a diamond breaks
with one hard blow

you only have to find
the line of weakness

*

We press our hearts
against the bed to keep
from hearing them

*

It stops in a cold room in Brooklyn
in a language I can't understand

I take off my rings
and hold my palms together
like a small boat

you lift the folded paper over them
you look down into water

there is no end to it
it falls
in my shaking hands

LETTERS FROM THE SNOW

1

All day the snow
like a fine curtain of salt
keeps me from seeing where I am

I go into myself
under the white drifts
eating the cold

are you still
dazed by the light
we reflect from each other?

Your green eyes sprout
like the end of winter
next to the fire

flames sing out of the sweet
wood and we dissolve
take shape dissolve

again my arms
dig under the snow
making a tunnel for my heart

I set it deep in the frozen earth
where it thumps like a tail
can you hear it so many nights away?

2

My stomach is flat as the sky
and the sky is a wall of snow
without any windows

I can't get over it
I have only my thin
breath here inside

the ground swells forward
gripping the house
and ice moves down

across the doors
sealing them tight
this is the long cold sleep

after the mind's death
when even the light
is exhausted

I grope for it
under the sill
but my arms lock over my own ribs

if only you'd speak
if only you'd shovel back
the dark

3

At dawn a pink light
covers my shadow on the snow
something that's still alive

moves under it
the whole field shines
through rose-tinted glass

as if we believed
in heaven or anything after
there's a jewelled scarab

where my heart should be
I sweep the snow
from the porch

wrapping a scarf around my face
under the wool my own breath
enters me

THE WORDS

As if I could almost
taste them in my mouth sometimes
I listen only to the words
you don't say

they never tell me the time
or make decisions
they do not explain about rising prices
or the cost of sugar

they have no sound
and cannot be used in an argument
small talk in the kitchen
keeps out of their way

listened for with my whole mind
I hear only their absence
they will not stop
or start anything

in what dream
what circle of memory
where in consecutive reason
do they hide

there's a room in my head
that opens a door
the room is the listener
and the silence that fills it

is the down quilt we draw
over our heads in winter
we can lie still in that warmth
without asking questions

someone will come to the room
the phone will ring
voices will rise through the wall
of the next apartment

we won't hear them
only the echo of the words you don't say
like the afterglow of loving
both empty and full

or the wet tip of a leaf
after the first rain
from which a clear drop of water
falls.

LOVING

There is a tiny wind in our room
where the fan hums
it moves the hands of the clock
like the fine hairs on your back
in every direction
we are going nowhere

all day we swam in the sea
to learn how water
lifts us from our lives
waves that we kept repeating

wherever we are
there are things we can count on
when I wake before dawn
the room is already light

III Starting Over

STARTING OVER

All day the geese fly south
in their old departures

nights when you sleep
among the dead
your hair keeps growing
out of your skin

nothing is casual
sometimes
you feel like swimming away
inside yourself
as if the time and place
already converged

if you go forward long enough
you'll come around
to the back door

the world is full of chances
to miss
even if the key fits
you mustn't go in

this is where you
                                begin

THE WAY

So this is the way
you leave the old country
where they're practising awareness
in the hot tubs
at Big Sur.

So this is the way
you leave the mother
tongue that stays
in the mouth that feeds it
but keeps quiet.

You can't learn two
landscapes in one
life he said
or a language
to put them in.

Picasso couldn't
learn arithmetic
because the number 7
looked like a nose
upside down.

So this is the way
you stand on your head
in Jerusalem: the wind
is the sea at Point Lobos
beating against the rocks.

LOOKING AT HENRY MOORE'S ELEPHANT SKULL ETCHINGS IN JERUSALEM DURING THE WAR

It wants to be somewhere else
remembering anything somewhere
private where it can lie down

floating in the warm belly
of the Dead Sea

so that the skull keeps
growing in the room

and the loose skin

until the whole head sees
its feet

from a great distance.

*

Heavy as earth is heavy
under its own weight

it's the same skin
wrinkled on the back of hills

grey in the early morning
on the Jericho Road.

*

The brain scooped out of it
lets in the light
we knew at the beginning

when our eyes were dazzled

pushed
without wanting to be pushed

out of the dark.

*

The mind of the elephant
has nothing to lose

*

I was begging you
not to go
when you closed the door

and left me
watching the skull's
round openings

the eyelids gone.

*

There are caverns
under our feet
with rivers running deep in them.

They hide
in the sides of cliffs
at Rosh Hanikra
where the sea breaks in.

There is a way to enter
if you remember
where you came from

how to breathe under water
make love in a trap.

*

Step over the small bones
lightly when you feel them
tripping your feet.

*

Fear hangs over your shoulder
like a gun it digs in my arm

but the live head knows
that the eyes get used to darkness

fingers learn how to read
the signs they touch.

*

Ditches where bones stand up
and shake their fists at us

sons in the shadows
and the shadows flattened
like grass rolled over

one-eyed Cyclops
slit of a concrete bunker
we prowl through
looking for flowers.

*

We are going down a long slide
into the secret chamber
we bought our tickets for the ride

the passage is narrow
and we can't find ourselves
in the trick mirrors

we lie down in the fetal position
back to back
each of us in his own eye socket

marvelous holes
the mind looked out of
filling with dust.

*

My lips on the small
rise of forehead above your eyes

mouths of the women in Ramallah
who spit when the soldiers go by

huge head of an infant
shoved out of the birth canal

faces stretched over us like tents
wet bandages over burns

and the white skull balder
than rock under the smile.

*

If the smooth joining of the bone
makes arches from here to there

if the intricate structure yields
arms resting desert landscapes mother and child

if the thin membranes and the thick
weep in the naked bone

then the whole elephant can rise up
out of its flesh

as in the torso of Apollo

something is pulsing
in the vacant skull

making us change.

*

I don't want to stand
on our balcony with the lights out
black buildings
street lamps
and headlights turned off

and nothing
against the sky

the stars get closer
but it's not the same
as what you plug in.

*

There's an elephant inside me
crowding me out
he sees Jerusalem
through my eyes my skin
is stretched tight
over the elephant's skin his wrinkles
begin to break through
I taste the coarse hairs
crowding the back of my mouth
I fall down gagging over my four feet
my nose turns into a tongue with nostrils

it starts to grow.

*

I see bodies in the morning kneel
over graves and bodies under them
the skin burned off
their bones laid out in all the cold
tunnels under the world.

There is a photograph in the next room
of a dead child
withered against its mother
between the dry beans of her breasts

there is no blood
under the shrunk skin

their skulls are already visible.

*

The elephants come after us
in herds now

they will roll over us
like tanks

we are too sad to move

our skulls
much smaller than theirs
begin to shine.

RERUNS

Whether you think of it
or not it's there
the face

whose name you've forgotten
haven't we met before?
The voices

go on speaking after you
switch them off
no and no

and yes and yes wanting
to have it all ways
even now.

*

We still hear them shoveling
the earth in his grave
so many people

we can't look down we can't
choose what to forget
when we're asleep

*

Last night you shifted into reverse
and drove backward
over the bridge

like a film rewinding you raced
back at the oncoming traffic
the cars got huge

in the rear-view mirror I screamed
stop but nothing
came out of my throat

DINOSAUR TRACKS IN BEIT ZAYIT

for Iris and Michael Wade

How there is anything so old
we can't imagine
anyone not there
to see them

three fingers
out of touch with each other

scars under my sole
like an old cut starting
to hurt again

when I put my foot
over his foot
I move in the same direction.

*

Everything dies in its own language
even before we find the name
and we remember only
what we can put together

what do I know about
pain in the bones of an old man
or those feet
always having to risk how far to go.

*

Next to the broken stones
in a small clearing
the sky is pale
as if it never got over the long night

and the white dust that gathered
where they fell
comes like sleep over my eyes

if I keep walking over the earth's rim
I'll disappear.

*

In less than the time it takes
to get from one life to another
we move closer together

I want to say to you
where are the children

the wind can't get in
where our shoulders touch.

*

Someone is digging next to her front door
she is planting a rose garden
her spade hits rock
she scoops the earth away
uncovering footprints

she thinks about everything
under her going
somewhere it doesn't arrive

at night when everyone's sleeping
she hears the silence of the world.

TAKE ANYTHING

1

I know a beautiful woman
with frugal eyes
who has written a book on Pain.
She tells me about the privilege
as if it were money.
The privilege of pain.
If you don't have it,
how will you know its absence?

Take anything
and imagine its absence:
the house we go back to
every night, a rock
too heavy to be moved,
fish jumping in the pond.

I put myself in the window
looking across the rock pile
to the pond. The house
is gone the rock is gone
the fish are gone. Even the pond
where we looked at ourselves
in each other.

But we are here.
I feel your breath along my tongue.
Something enters my head
like the fish splashing and the pond
breaking and mending, breaking
and mending in the sun.

2

At the end of summer an east wind
blows from the desert
like a visible flame, blue
under the smoky light,
sucking the moisture from the air
that shrivels around our heads.

The fresh mint growing in the pots
wilts and gets spindly.
We blame everything on the weather.
If you don't feel it, you haven't
lived here long enough, they say.

The heat drifts out the door
when the moon rises.

3

Swimming in Puget Sound at night
when we were children, our skin glowed
in the phosphorescent water.
We shook the light off as we ran
shivering to the great log fire.
The driftwood sang like jungles,
and we danced ourselves warm around it,
close as we dared, and closer
till I slipped on the wet sand.
Somebody pulled me out and rolled me
in blankets while the sparks
rose over me like stars
and the smoke whitened my white lips.

4

We saw the bronze head of Hadrian
covered with centuries of clay
the day they found it
in a plowed field. The curls
were tight around his neat head
catching the sun. The tip
of his perfect nose shone
through the grit.

To test a rumor, Hadrian chained
a line of slaves and threw them
into the Dead Sea, proving
a man could drown but not sink
in those oily waters.

Can you imagine the long pain
privilege for anyone drowning
in his own death, wanting to sink?

My mother taking six years to die.
The last time I saw her there were
bruises all over her shoulders
where they strapped her in the chair.

5

Now at the bottom of the world
the Dead Sea moans
and clots of tar rise to the surface
like rotting bodies. We watch them
spread into greasy stains.

This is the place, you say,
as if pointing to light
in the old paintings, how it
comes from a source itself unlit
preceding the painter.
If you don't see it,
how will you know its absence?

Take anything unburied
from the old life when they all ran
screaming up the beach. Pain
moves from the center slowly
like the sound of a plucked string
dwindling into space.

I strain to hear it
as I keep floating face up
in the salt.

MEETING

I never can tell when the top of the world
is blowing away below me
where the west ends and the east begins
or clouds and ice

or what I might do
if there were white arms sinking
out of the sky calling for help.

And now it is you who are traveling
still in the false world of children
who hear what they can't see:
those sounds behind the partition
in the dark.

I can't explain why I'm afraid
of events we prepare for
of meeting again
in the city of ultimate meetings
bull's-eye of earth and heaven
fixed point of Moriah

where we'll stare at each other
across the rock.

If time's not linear as you insist
we're locked into rings
repeating ourselves
and even airplanes go nowhere
with marvelous speed.

We all have places to get to
and you'll discover what happened
is not what you heard

that even the spring is ambivalent
here with the hot wind
breaking suddenly to cold.

We have outlived our expectations
though I still dream of the house
I grew up in
where the two aunts waited
for husbands who never came.

A sickness is creeping into the bark
of pine trees so they die
faster than we can cure them

and I don't know when you touch ground
unfasten your seat belt
and climb down into the bushes
whether you'll see the ram.

THE MOUNTAIN

1

In the morning I am alone in the icy room
everyone has gone to climb the mountain
the only sound is the noise in my head
machine of my anger or my fear
that won't shut off
the wind keeps cranking it.

My daughter has fled to the mountain
a piece of her dress in my hand
it is green
and I hold it next to my ear
to stop the wind.

What she took out of me
was not what I meant to give.
She hears strange voices.
I dream she's the child I grew up with
kneeling beside her hamsters
soft things she cared for
cradling them in her hands.

I want to make my words into a hamster
and nest them in her palms
to be sorry again
when she falls out of the tree
and breaks her arm.

She runs to an empty house
with her own prophets
they sit shoulder to shoulder
waiting for the sky to open
they can already see through a tiny crack
where the path begins.

2

Yesterday we saw how roots of mangroves
suck the warm sea at the desert's edge
and keep the salt
the leaves are white
and flaky as dead skin.
My ankles swell.
I must be drowning in my own brine.

A Bedouin woman stands veiled
in the ruined courtyard
there's a well
a hole in the ground
where she leads the camel by a rope
I watch her fill the bucket
and the camel drinks
lifting its small shrewd head
rinsing its teeth with a swollen tongue.

The woman is covered in black
her body her head her whole face black
except for the skin around her eyes.

My daughter watches me watch her
with the same eyes.

She picks up a handful of rocks
and hits the camel
shrieking she strikes it
over and over to make it move.

I am alone in the icy room
everyone has gone to climb the mountain
the only sound is the woman
chasing the camel with the rocks.

I look out at the dry river bed.
I let her go.

THINKING ABOUT THE FUTURE OF JERUSALEM

There is a black thread
winding around my legs
as on a spool strong as the thread
that's used to sew on gold buttons.
I can't break it off with my teeth.

That's what I get
for walking around in this city
with its excess of wars
and walls that go down deeper
than we can uncover.

I'm like a child
who lives only with adults.
They take her everywhere
in grown-up company
where she has to behave

when all the time
she wants to be singing
to herself or chasing
lizards running in and out
of the tall grass.

I have never seen a rock crumble
under the weight of history
or a life crumble
under the weight of fear.
And if I can only get

my legs untied I'll stand
in line with all the people
who eat too much at buffet tables
and keep filling filling
their plates with more.

THE NEXT STEP

To make what is simple
out of the common
root   to tell
of the things around us
in the light
each morning the edge again
bright surface of stones

or after the long hot summer
first clouds
filling the empty sky

we are all waking
even behind our closed eyes
even behind the doors
still locked at dawn

downstairs the neighbor's child
is crying again

the cramp of hunger
extended passage
out of ourselves to take
the next step

can we invent a new thing rounder
than the wheel invent
a new word
perfect as wing
or space it moves through

maybe we lived before
in these same rooms
the past we never break out of
shards in the dust
still under the floor

each place we come to
where we've already been
we look for pieces
stories told over and over
that finally matter

families gather
again the grapes
are sticky with flies
and summer's finished

the year begins
with apples
as though the world begins

and love

only to speak of it
while it goes on

Rosh Hashana 5738
The Jewish New Year

PITT POETRY SERIES

Ed Ochester, General Editor

Dannie Abse, *Collected Poems*
Adonis, *The Blood of Adonis*
Jack Anderson, *The Invention of New Jersey*
Jack Anderson, *Toward the Liberation of the Left Hand*
Jon Anderson, *Death & Friends*
Jon Anderson, *In Sepia*
Jon Anderson, *Looking for Jonathan*
John Balaban, *After Our War*
Gerald W. Barrax, *Another Kind of Rain*
Robert Coles, *A Festering Sweetness: Poems of American People*
Leo Connellan, *First Selected Poems*
Michael Culross, *The Lost Heroes*
Fazil Hüsnü Daglarca, *Selected Poems*
James Den Boer, *Learning the Way*
James Den Boer, *Trying to Come Apart*
Norman Dubie, *Alehouse Sonnets*
Norman Dubie, *In the Dead of the Night*
Odysseus Elytis, *The Axion Esti*
John Engels, *Blood Mountain*
John Engels, *The Homer Mitchell Place*
John Engels, *Signals from the Safety Coffin*
Abbie Huston Evans, *Collected Poems*
Brendan Galvin, *The Minutes No One Owns*
Brendan Galvin, *No Time for Good Reasons*
Gary Gildner, *Digging for Indians*
Gary Gildner, *First Practice*
Gary Gildner, *Nails*
Gary Gildner, *The Runner*
Mark Halperin, *Backroads*
Patricia Hampl, *Woman Before an Aquarium*
Michael S. Harper, *Dear John, Dear Coltrane*
Michael S. Harper, *Song: I Want a Witness*
John Hart, *The Climbers*
Samuel Hazo, *Blood Rights*
Samuel Hazo, *Once for the Last Bandit: New and Previous Poems*
Samuel Hazo, *Quartered*
Gwen Head, *The Ten Thousandth Night*
Gwen Head, *Special Effects*
Milne Holton and Graham W. Reid, eds., *Reading the Ashes: An Anthology of the Poetry of Modern Macedonia*

Milne Holton and Paul Vangelisti, eds., *The New Polish Poetry: A Bilingual Collection*
David Huddle, *Paper Boy*
Shirley Kaufman, *The Floor Keeps Turning*
Shirley Kaufman, *From One Life to Another*
Shirley Kaufman, *Gold Country*
Abba Kovner, *A Canopy in the Desert: Selected Poems*
Paul-Marie Lapointe, *The Terror of the Snows: Selected Poems*
Larry Levis, *Wrecking Crew*
Jim Lindsey, *In Lieu of Mecca*
Tom Lowenstein, tr., *Eskimo Poems from Canada and Greenland*
Archibald MacLeish, *The Great American Fourth of July Parade*
Peter Meinke, *The Night Train and The Golden Bird*
James Moore, *The New Body*
Carol Muske, *Camouflage*
Gregory Pape, *Border Crossings*
Thomas Rabbitt, *Exile*
Belle Randall, *101 Different Ways of Playing Solitaire and Other Poems*
Ed Roberson, *Etai-Eken*
Ed Roberson, *When Thy King Is A Boy*
Eugene Ruggles, *The Lifeguard in the Snow*
Dennis Scott, *Uncle Time*
Herbert Scott, *Groceries*
Richard Shelton, *The Bus to Veracruz*
Richard Shelton, *Of All the Dirty Words*
Richard Shelton, *The Tattooed Desert*
Richard Shelton, *You Can't Have Everything*
Gary Soto, *The Elements of San Joaquin*
Gary Soto, *The Tale of Sunlight*
David Steingass, *American Handbook*
David Steingass, *Body Compass*
Tomas Tranströmer, *Windows & Stones: Selected Poems*
Alberta T. Turner, *Learning to Count*
Alberta T. Turner, *Lid and Spoon*
Marc Weber, *48 Small Poems*
David P. Young, *Sweating Out the Winter*

Poetry by Shirley Kaufman

The Floor Keeps Turning
1969 United States Award of the International Poetry Forum and National Council on the Arts Selection

Gold Country

Looking at Henry Moore's Elephant Skull Etchings in Jerusalem During the War

Translations

My Little Sister, translated from the Hebrew of Abba Kovner. In *Abba Kovner and Nelly Sachs: Selected Poems.*

A Canopy in the Desert, translated from the Hebrew of Abba Kovner.

The Light of Lost Suns, translated from the Hebrew of Amir Gilboa.